HEALING AND WITCHCRAFT

THE MERRY WAY WITCH

This is a work of fiction. Names, characters, places, organizations, corporations, locales and so forth are a product of the author's imagination, or if real, used fictitiously. Any resemblance to a person, living or dead, is entirely coincidental.

CONTENTS

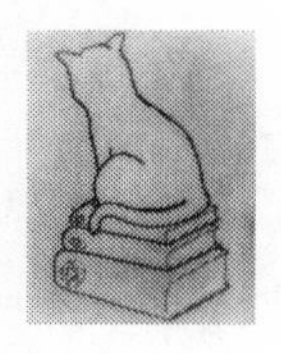

PREFACE

The Merry Way Witch reveals how she moved out of the negative frequency of low self-esteem, into authentic expression and healing as taught to her through Mother Nature, specifically, the very essence of Witchcraft.

Healing and Witchcraft in a Conformist World is her book of shadows, a guide to unconventional healing methods that include screaming out one's pain to connect with core identity, voice and authenticity, adopting a limitless mindset after reinterpreting the confines of modern psychotherapy and infusing wisdom from the Goddess Hecate.

The creation of *Healing and Witchcraft in a Conformist World* inspired the need to support souls who believe they are alone or do not belong to the modern world; it is a statement of profound awareness and encouragement for a soul's healing journey which can be supremely supported through the tenets of Witchcraft. Celebrate your non-conventional and non-conformist presence in this lifetime, for you have never been alone, and this book is just one way to bring about the support, acceptance, and peace that you deserve.

This book was written with all who comes across it in mind. It is a small book filled with earthy and other realm wisdom that, hopefully, will ease the anxiety you feel about being a Spiritual Witch—Beautiful Being in this modern world of ours. This book is not a basic Witchcraft 101 text; that you can find anywhere these days, and, dare I say it, better written than I could have attempted. This is a collection of personal healing and metaphysical tales which graced me with the wisdom to bridge the gap between the need to fit into the world and forge my own spiritual, badass self. And now I am passing that wisdom to you as you embrace the essence of Witchcraft and the path of healing; a path that I feel goes hand in hand.

As always, I want you to read what is written in these next twenty-five chapters with discernment. The contents of this book are here to reveal, inform and support; I am not here to promote a single way of approaching and living your life. I write as I speak, and hopefully the one truism you are sure to gain from this healing manifesta is a clearer perspective of who I am, and I predict you will ascertain we are not so different from each other, not at all.

With Respect,
The Merry Way Witch

ONE

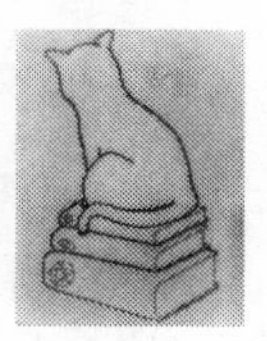

AH, IT'S THE WITCHES LIFE FOR ME, AND NOW YOU...

There is a belief that if you are attracted to Witchcraft in this lifetime it is because you carried the knowledge of the Craft with you from previous existences. Do we know that for sure? Of course not, but I can tell you that most, if not all, of whom I have known to take on this path of nature-loving goodness do fall right into it as though it is their second skin.

It is completely normal to feel nervous about following your heart down the path of Nature Worship, Paganism, Witchcraft or Wicca. You are not alone in your apprehension. I had a friend who once borrowed a few of my Pagan books only to return them after a week because of the impending doom she felt. She was convinced she would be "arrested" for embracing the ways of Witchcraft. The damage encasing the essence of what Witchcraft truly is, is palpable, and in time you will move past any inherited and limited thinking, knowing what has been said about the practices of Witches is not even close to the truth of what *we* actually stand for. But fear, like everything else, is a process, one to face and overcome. No one who believes in the beauty of nature and stands within its power ready to learn is inherently evil; never was, never will be.

There might be something else you may have discovered about yourself—besides your amazing interest in the occult. Perhaps you think you are a freak, a loner, perhaps you suffer from anxiety, or maybe you just don't believe you are as good as those around you. Others may have told you that you are strange, or maybe you see this belief in the faces of the world as you try so hard to move through it, desperately trying not to give away the fact that you don't belong.

Well, to this I say, you're right. You don't belong. You were not born to swim upstream with the other fishes; you were born to move against the tide of "the norm." Your interest in Witchcraft just proves that. There have been many generations of fear surrounding the mystery that is Witchcraft. You are picking up on that fear, as there is a more than small chance you are a sensitive soul who feels and sees what many don't.

Is being sensitive a curse? Fucking right it is. You must stand and believe in all that you are. Stop comparing yourself to a world that still burns women because they do not understand *her* power (and yes, this is still a modern day occurrence).

The first method in moving down the road of not comparing yourself to others is accepting that there is something a little different about you. Yes, they know, and who cares if they do? Perhaps your family thinks you're a little "touched"; mine did. But, try as I might, I never did fit into the world of the nine-to-five worker, scheduled family vacation every year existence. Now, to be clear, there is nothing wrong with this lifestyle. I myself was jealous of this way of being for so long. If you choose this lifestyle, you'll be happy, and if you are a happy Witch with a nine-to-five job and a planned vacation, AMAZING! Go be you (and take me with you)! But if this lifestyle choice doesn't appeal to you, that's perfectly fine too. This world is designed to include all sorts of different visions of living with different experiences—but don't tell the Patriarchy. They're not too keen on diversity!

So, your first lesson: stand in your own power without comparing yourself to those who might be limited by their own fear. Your job in this lifetime is to face and incorporate your own fear. Taking on anyone else's fear will only keep you from your destiny, which is to evolve into the best, most complete, kick-ass Witch there is!

TWO

COMING OUT OF THE WITCH'S CLOSET

Once upon a time in a private space somewhere on the East Coast, a friend disclosed to me that she was a Witch, then promptly declared *I* could not be a true Witch because those in the city where we lived knew me as one. To this, I say she was wrong on two levels. Firstly, I was always careful who I told my business to; so, no, not everyone knew of my Witchiness, and the idea you are not a true Witch because you are not completely cloaked in anonymity is ridiculous. NEVER let anyone tell you that you are not authentic because you did not subscribe to their very specific projections about authenticity or Witchcraft protocol.

BE discerning, be, be discerning…

It is, however, extremely fruitful to not declare your love of the Craft randomly to a room full of strangers who would not understand your attraction to Witchcraft. Even though I was careful who I confided my Witch life to, I was lucky enough to be in a small community that was Pagan and Wiccan heavy. I lived and trained among this amazing tribe. And even though I am not Wiccan, which is a recognized religion—I'm more of a find-your-own-path-through-Witchcraft kind of girl (okay, I'll admit I'm also not great with rules, hence going the Witchcraft route)—I believe I was discerning about my beliefs and interests. But I'm not exempt from being misunderstood, even though I was careful.

One year I believed it was time to tattoo a pentacle upon my back, a symbol of supreme protection only nature can offer. After the tattoo was completed, my best friend and I went to a local watering hole. I got chatting with a very open-minded person, or so I thought. After talking for quite a while I showed her my tattoo. She then excused herself only to appear in front of my friend to ask him why he was friends with a Satan worshipper, to which he replied, "I'm not. Go home and get informed." Lesson learned; even I, a medium and empath of all things, misjudged someone's level of openness, and I would never make that mistake again.

Now, I'm not suggesting you become guarded, turn into a hermit and only talk to your cat familiar from now on, but telling someone who won't understand your intentions will only cause your own power to diminish. Why put yourself in a position from which you will be forced to defend yourself? You should never have to defend yourself, because there is NOTHING suspect about your beliefs.

One word here about Satanism... Satanism has evolved and grown from the very specific and one-dimensional understanding of what it once was, so being compared to a Satanist is actually in many ways a compliment. But, for the sake of keeping on track, please respect your space and your beliefs; not everyone needs to know you have an altar in your room. My dry cleaner didn't need to know! But he sure found out one sunny afternoon when a friend who was picking up her dry cleaning outed me as a Witch. The owner asked how I was doing, and her answer, "Oh, you mean the Witch, yes, she's fine!" No, No. No.

My wonderful interactions with my dry cleaner, which usually revolved around me asking after his family when dropping off my vintage jackets to be cleaned, does not automatically mean he needs to be privy to my Witchy ways. That is the very thing I said to my friend, so she understood that outing me in the future would be entirely frowned upon by myself and my cat familiar, the only creature I believed had my back! Ha! I jest...

Do make sure any social faux pas such as the one above is corrected as soon as possible. I was stern but fair with my friend when I insisted she never out me again in public. She did not know to out me would be a problem and, therefore, thought nothing of her actions, and that's the point. Not everyone understands the prejudice or the misunderstandings we incur. And some might think it's cool to be a Witch. Well, it isn't cool to be outed. You offer the information about yourself, never another (unless they have express permission from you).

Being open about your beliefs is wonderful. We have had many open Witches since the 1960s and 1970s, both in the UK and the US, paving the way for a new generation to stand strong in our beliefs. After all, if we were all hidden from the world, the public might still hold a rather perverse and incorrect opinion of us, and we can't have that!

As always, I believe trusting your intuition and striking a balance is key when navigating the social aspect of your Witchy life. One last observation here, you have probably noticed I have published this book under the name of *The Merry Way Witch*. I have, however, written rather significantly for Witchcraft publications over the years using my real name. I did say I believed in balance. I also believe that it's fun to invoke my anonymity clause; even I, on occasion, love to cloak myself from the world, but not too much...

You'll find your own path, and gauge correctly how you will operate your good self in the big bad world, being your big bad self! And that's how it should be.

THREE

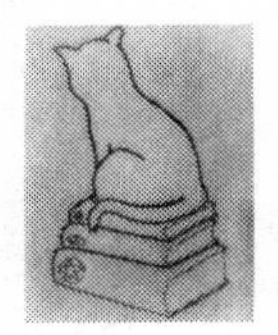

THE BEAUTIFUL MESS THAT IS SPIRITUAL HEALING

The question I am asked most from non-Witches in my healing and mediumship practice is, should everyone seek out spiritual healing? My simple answer is "NO." It's a blunt answer, I know, but it doesn't make it any less true.

The way I see it is that you have the beautiful chance to live a profound life in this world of ours, and within that understanding of the world you'll come to create your own version of reality based on your thoughts and desires. But not all want or need this version of living.

I was a spiritually inclined child; a daydreamer and Magic maker, although I had no actual words for it back then. But I never came to the work I do with open arms; far from it. I came to it because my life was no longer manageable. I couldn't stand crowds or raised voices. People's energy would make me sick and I didn't know why. I didn't have enough sense of self or knowledge to block or protect myself from the negativity out there. I had heard the term "empath" and figured to some degree everyone was, so what? The worse of it was that I began to dumb down the pain of being so sensitive, sometimes with alcohol, but sometimes I just ran and then panicked because I didn't know what was happening to me. I finally stopped and realized if I was going to have any chance of an actual life I needed to train and hone in on my gifts.

However, at that point I had nothing left to lose, so, you could argue, there was no courage required to step up and join a nine-month course that would very quickly change my life in profound ways I didn't know possible.

I will be clear; my life as a sensitive didn't get less painful as I began to honor my gifts. There were raw moments, messy moments, painful moments where my old life fell away from me, and that was confusing and lonely. To heal yourself takes great courage, and it's terribly uneasy and untidy work. Please don't expect your life not to fall apart, or at the very least never be the same again. The work of self-discovery takes commitment because with all the teachers you seek out to help you (and you should—everyone needs guidance and support), in the end, the work is yours and only yours to truly take on.

Being self-aware is not for the faint-hearted, and not everyone wants to be faced with their own darkness. So not everyone should seek out spiritual healing and Magic, however—and there is a huge "however" here—if you are one of the brave few who chooses to take on the responsibility of their own energy of light and dark, there is a peacefulness that comes with knowing your soul, and I can tell you, the blissfulness that peace provides is worth staying brave for.

Being privy to a constant flow of unconditional love changes everything; your energy, relationships, and your life. So for all you brave, beautiful souls out there who have decided to walk in your own light, congrats! This path will be uniquely strange, wonderful, precious, precocious, and memorable. Move forward into your new life, and seek out what you will never be able to find in the mundane world... Go be free...

FOUR

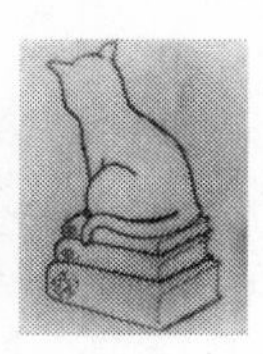

THE ILLUMINATION OF MAGIC

Whenever you read this, no matter what time of the month, the energy of the moon—whether waning, waxing, new or full—is upon us. Moon Magic is my favorite kind of Magic; after all, who doesn't love bathing in moonbeams? Now, for all of you out there who are wondering *does Magic work? Should I be afraid of it? And, if it does work, how does it work?*

I am here for you. And for all of you who believe that bathing in the light of the moon is for the new age movement (SO not crazy about that phase, ahhhhh), I have something to say to you too.

Everyone is made up of energy, and each of us produces and releases energy, so be responsible for yours! Magic is energy, and learning how to work with energy—your own, others', and the energy of the universe at large—will only help you understand yourself and the beautiful world we live in. Magic, in all of its various forms, brings us in contact with the truest, most innocent parts of ourselves. Unfortunately, though, people over hundreds of years have been told that utilizing the energy of Magic is inherently evil. This is a fear based thought. I'm not going to point out the obvious when it comes to fear-based thoughts and what jail-like limitations it bestows upon you. I always say, "Fear is its own keeper!" (So, I'll leave *what fear does to you if you let it into your heart* for another time.)

I will say, though, whether we realize it or not, most of us use Magic on a day-to-day basis. When you blow out your birthday candles and make a wish; that's Magic! On the hour train ride to work every morning when you watch the houses zoom by and wish for a different kind of life (perhaps one where you don't have to spend an hour getting to work every morning), you are streamlining your energy and shifting into different versions of what you could be in your own mind. Now just send that intention out, out, and away! Creating Magic is merely taking your desire and adding energy and focus, strengthening your original thought and desire, so it has a more direct route to the stars, so to speak.

So, My Lovelies, off you pop. Go grab that crystal, that meaningful necklace your mother gave you, or any type of object that already holds powerful and ancestral energy, and work with it to manifest your dreams. Be still in your thoughts, be clear about what you want, visualize the outcome, and stay strong in only giving your dreamy outcome positive energy. And remember the golden rule—always work in accordance with the universe and what will be for your highest good!

Happy Manifesting!

FIVE

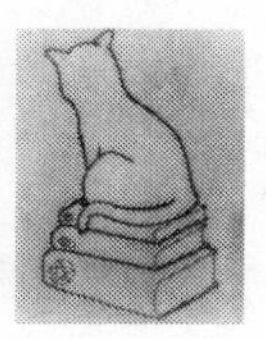

THE PRACTICAL MIND VERSUS THE INTUITIVE MIND

I have never considered myself one who lived a clear and productive life, although I will say my time on this earth has never been boring!

I, for one, often mistook drama for cultivating an exciting or deep existence, and I often mistook a practical mindset for a mature and necessary trait to live a full and beautiful life. I was, of course, quite wrong on both counts!

Now, to be clear, I'm not suggesting embracing the essence of practicality will get you nowhere, so pay your bills (then treat yourself to a cocktail of your choice). In that vein, I'm also not suggesting you must run from your life because "you can't handle it anymore." I have actually done this many times, and have fallen on my feet (eventually), but not without moving through useless struggles I believed I needed to face because it was a necessary aspect of "living free."

The only person who made my life much more complicated then it needed to be was ME. I, alone, believed life was about fighting for what I wanted, and I also mistakenly believed that struggle was a necessary factor in negotiating the terms of my true desires: "if it ain't worth fighting for, it ain't worth having." Well, I'm here to tell you that, unfortunately, AGAIN, I had it all wrong. Yes, I'm admitting I was really, really, really terrible at living a successful life, mainly because I didn't know I deserved one.

I surrounded myself with people who believed not everyone deserved love or success. I let people into my life who were dramatic, fearful, and angry, blaming their pain on everyone instead of looking within. Not only did I let these people into my life, but I also shared my life with them—I sought them out and I believed in their fears until those fears finally melded into mine.

I moved (very unglamorously, I might add) between living a super efficient, bland, yet extremely practical life, doing what I needed to do to be an upstanding citizen, then blowing up and running from all my responsibilities because I was drowning under the pressures of life. I had NO sense of balance, and there were no examples of successful and balanced people around me, so I continued in this hamster-wheeled existence until one final day... the day I dared myself to do things differently.

I dared to look at and unravel MY own pain, and I began to listen to my own heart and what IT desired. It was a rocky existence to begin with. Even though I sometimes listened to my heart and that small voice inside telling me I didn't need this job or this situation in my life, I still occasionally opted to ignore that voice, only to be met with unsatisfying outcomes. However, over time I started seeing that my world was changing. I took small chances at first. I finally began relying on my inner voice, and I began to judge each situation according to what my intuition thought best. Fearful situations and similar typed people started to fall away from my life, even though I fought to keep them a part of me (of course I did. They were familiar).

I began making decisions that confused people. That was

when I knew I was leaving my former life behind and evoking a new way of being. Then I began to take bigger chances based on my desire to be of service, and to truly embrace my soul's mission. I began to trust that my intuition knew better than my practical mind, which only wanted to play it safe and stay small so no one would hurt us.

Then one day an incredible occurrence happened. I began not to care that I couldn't be understood or defined by some. I was no longer trying to "make it" or "fit in." Instead, I was living a life that was beginning to reflect my need to make this world a better place, full of truth, wisdom, and beauty. When my practical mind came into play offering up a situation that would amount to me playing it safe, I now had the courage to say, "NO. Thanks for the option, but I'm choosing differently."

Living up to your potential takes a vast amount of courage, and it took me many, many, many, many (you get the point here) years to develop that courage. But once it struck I embraced it and began a whole new level of existence.

Your homework this week, should you decide to take on this task, is to listen to that small voice instructing you of your heart's desire. Are the needs of your inner voice reflected in your actual life? What could you do to bring more of your beauty and knowledge into this world of ours? Is your true potential unfolding before you?

See what your inner voice says when you ask it the above questions. Sit with your incredible intuition, that, believe it or not, wants the best for you. Dare to be great. Start small—no one is asking you to be Superman overnight, but if you want to wear a cape to work, I say GO FOR IT!

Live! Live from your heart. It will never steer you wrong!

SIX

THE AMAZING EFFECTS OF A DEDICATED MAGICAL MINDSET

There are few schools of thought on the use of Magic. When conversing with a Wiccan man at a weekend Pagan gathering, I was informed he was vehemently against any Pagan, no matter the spell, doing Magic. He believed spellwork was a specific and intentional energy that interfered with the natural process of life. For instance, if you do a spell to win over a potential boss at a job interview, you are sabotaging (with Magical intent) someone else's chances for that same position, someone who might have been more qualified, yet were not called to use Magic to increase their chance for success.

Many Witches, however, believe Magic and spellwork is a divine right of the modern Witch. This quandary to use or not to use Magic, of course, is always up to you. Should you decide to be Magical, be prepared to make mistakes; as long as they are not as epic as those found in the movie *The Craft*, you, and those around you, will be fine. You will, in time, be able to gather how your energy navigates within spellcraft and therefore set your own boundaries and limits on what and whom you will practice on.

I have always believed conducting a spell that compromises someone else's free will is a no-no, but I know many talented Witches who do just that, and they sleep very soundly at night. Also, I'm not a huge believer in binding another from doing harm, or cursing them, but there is a Witchcraft movement that exists to bring down the Capitalist elite, and free us all from the... fill in the many blanks here... that they are doing to this country, and indeed the world. Magic is powerful, and when combined with other Magic from those seeking the same desire and the same outcome, it is (more often than not) unstoppable. Again, you'll have to decide whether you are up for binding and cursing those who do harm to others, or you can watch the Magic unfold without judgment and keep that small inward smile of camaraderie for those badass Witches who are using their power in the most comprehensive way *they* see fit.

However you decide to direct your energy in the form of Magic in the world, remember four grounded truisms that have never led me astray:

Always do Magic from a place of love, not fear. AND I'M SERIOUS about this; if you are afraid of your own power, or approach Magic with a fearful nature, that's the energy you are infusing into your spellwork. As already stated, fear is its own keeper. It manipulates truth and beauty in profound ways that never serve us. To truthfully infuse your power with pure energy and nature you will need to be present and have complete trust. You cannot hope to achieve such a feat if you hold fear in your heart. Fear disconnects us from everything, including our own authenticity. Incidentally, if you've designed a method to utilize fear within Magic, go you—but that's advanced spellwork, so let's just stick to the basics here.

Remember spellwork amplifies the energy inside of you, so if you want to be a kick-ass Magical Witch, know who you are. Face the darkness that can hold you back and bring you down seemingly out of nowhere, as our subconscious is apt to do. Have the courage to seek out teachers of this earthly realm and those who work outside of said realm. Be confident, knowing your heart has been exposed and broken, and you're still very much here and ready to learn. Vulnerability pushes arrogance out of its way, and that's the correct attitude to have when approaching Magic. So, to recap: be confident, humble, open, trusting, protecting, and grateful.

Make sure every aspect of your spellcraft reflects your clear and true intention.

Never go against your own moral code—and yes, you have one! The foundation of Witchcraft is thinking for yourself and creating your own version of the world we live in, so, do just that. If you don't like Ouija boards, don't mess around with them. Don't let anyone tell you that they are safe. They are for some, and, therefore, I know many Witches who successfully use these portals with incredible results, but that does not mean you must follow in their footsteps. Your relationship with the occult is just that, your relationship, so make sure no one tries to pull you out of your depth before you are ready. That's usually when the mystical shit hits the fan, and no one needs mystical shit on their hands. It doesn't wash off easily!

SEVEN

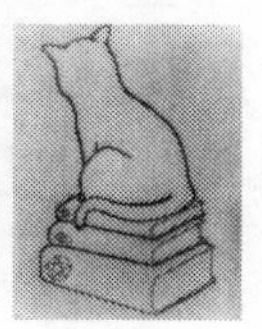

BASIC TOOLS FOR THE SUCCESSFUL WITCH

Every Witch's basic tool list will be a little different; again, there are no rules.

My personal picks are as follows: a familiar—mine is a cat who followed me home many years ago, and still hasn't left my side—and a cauldron—used by women for hundreds of years to make spells, potions, food, and energy. This amazing vessel is a must for any beautiful Witch, male or female. The cauldron is a direct link to the lineage of those who have come before, those who have shared the same faith, blood, and trauma.

So, if these words resonate with you, and you still don't have a cauldron on hand, go get one of your own. It doesn't matter whether your cauldron is new, and waiting to be integrated into your Magical practices, or, an antique cauldron which already possesses infused energy from another. Trust me, either way, you'll feel its power!

Candles for candle Magic play a huge part in my Witchy life. Candles, and fire itself, burns away the past and sets the tone for the future. Fire is a reminder we were once burnt and killed for our belief in nature, and yet we rose from the flames. And, finally, to add to my basic list of Witchcraft musts; herbs—simple kitchen herbs will do. The usual, lavender for luck and cellular healing, rosemary for memory and protection, and sage for cleansing and returning to center. I love a little patchouly oil for love, but not everyone can get down with the smell.

I will say here that collectively I believe most, if not all, Witches should possess a keen sense of smell to be able to sniff at, then reject, the bullshit life will try and pass off as truth, a profound sense of autonomy and self-worth, an open and beautiful mind, and a connection to your soul's development that surpasses what some here on earth settle for. Oh, and you'll need a grounded interior, one that does not lose themselves in the world's opinion of them; blending the personal and the collective elements of Witchcraft is a fun endeavor.

The rest, well, that's up to you! My only advice in pursuing the path of Witchcraft (other than what I have laid out above), is not to be fucking precious about it! Most beginner books will tell you to do things a certain way, and most of that advice is for your protection, but the energies you will be working with don't really care if you've bathed before spellwork or if you are eating a box of Corn Flakes while setting up your protective circle, so bring your brand of you to the Craft. Life shouldn't be taken too seriously. I believe that energy infused into your love of the Craft will push you extremely far.

So ride those broomsticks high above the clouds, and let everyone know you're a bad-ass-Witch-from-Hell (oh wait, maybe not from Hell, but, who knows, maybe you are...).

EIGHT

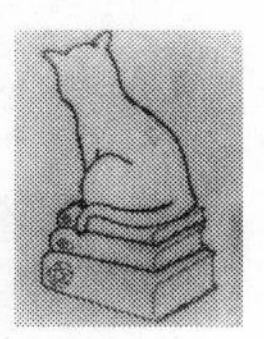

WITCHCRAFT AND THE DEVIL; A CHRISTIAN LOVE STORY

We all know that Christianity has, in the past, had a beef with Paganism, a beef of the biggest kind. It started by merging the Pagan Horned God, who was adorned by stag horns, into that of the Christian Devil. That way Christians could condemn the Pagan God and justify murdering those who honored his power. But we're not here to condemn those who have condemned, because we are ALL human beings.

There have been respectful, and mostly accurate, portrayals of Witches in modern society. Willow from *Buffy the Vampire Slayer* — yes, she went off the track a little, but it's Willow, so we couldn't fall out of love with her. The Halliwell Sisters won our hearts. I cried for a week when Prue died (ok, it wasn't a week, but, I was still affected). *Practical Magic*—special shout out to Alice Hoffman, you rock!—was a huge hit in my Witchy abode. Talking of houses, I don't know one Witch who doesn't want to live in the *Practical Magic* house! And, of course, *The Craft*, the film that demonstrated the complexity and reality of spellcraft, and who didn't love the Witch who owned the occult store; the only voice of sanity throughout the movie?

As stated, I am sure there are many (more than I featured above) somewhat accurate and flattering portrayals of Witchcraft, but unfortunately there are still many sources out there that spread the old propaganda. One documentary I watched recently, *The Haunting on Dice Road: The Hell House,* blamed the haunting on a woman who claimed to be an ordained Witch. There were witness accounts of men being bewitched, but no one could remember details of what occurred, if indeed anything actually did, in these bewitchings. Apparently, the Witch's house had strange markings upon it. Some were confirmed by a Catholic priest as being Satanic (as the "Witch" claimed to be too), but when I scoured the internet I could find no confirmation these were, in fact, Satanic markings. I am not privy to the information a priest has access to, and that is perhaps my point. So, again I say, BE DISCERNING. BE, BE, DISCERNING. ALWAYS do your own research and develop your own relationship to your own path as soon as you can. Take no information at face value. Don't allow old projections to interfere with your knowledge of the truth. The church changed the bible from "thou shalt not suffer a poisoner to live" to "thou shalt not suffer a Witch to live" in the Burning Times to justify the massacre of women and those who didn't meet the "standards" of the Christian faith—that OLD PROPAGANDA still exists! Don't stand for it!

I believe it is extremely important to understand the tenets of societal fear so we may release said fear and live (hopefully) beyond its grasp. Therefore, I was led to understand for myself the true nature of Lucifer, or Satan; after all, I have been accused too many times of harboring his intent from those who view Witchcraft as a threat, so why would I not discover his actual origin and what he *truly* stands for?

I found my research to be both enlightening and fascinating. The Christian accounts of Lucifer reduce him to a fallen angel who stood against God. Lucifer, then, was used to create a balance, and is the darkness to God's light. However, my research, which dates back to pre-biblical findings, brought me to the understanding that in fact Lucifer's human representation is much more complicated than merely being God's adversary. Yes, there is an aspect of duality to his presence, but instead of encompassing darkness, a representation of evil or human, basic desires, Lucifer represents the *unknown*. He is neither good nor bad, light nor dark; "Lucifer" *is* the void, a bridge between illumination and darkness, two very human modes of existence. "Lucifer's" void status allows for humans to project upon him. He is not the king of darkness. He has become a representative of evil because humans have created him in their own image for hundreds of years.

Lucifer is, and will always be, a scapegoat for the darkness that exists within each human. No beast bearing the number 666 actually exists in nature. There is no *one* being that can claim to preside over the totality of evil. True evil exists within humans and is mirrored in how we treat each other. It should be no wonder that the will and fears of the human race created Lucifer and gave him power through our own fear of what is not easily seen, our subconscious. The only method of exorcising him (pardon the pun) from our hearts is to truly comprehend that he is not an external threat; the darkness he represents is our own to examine. Personal and universal darkness should be acknowledged, healed and reintegrated, or it will compromise and erode our humanity.

Mark my words—even though I do not believe in the commonly known version of Lucifer, there is an entity behind that biblical mask, and he has great power. So, if you are looking to call on him, make sure you are ready to face all of your fears, as his presence will require you to equalize any darkness that might hold you back from becoming the full light filled human he desires you to become.

Lucifer's true identity can be found under the name of Heylal.

*For those of you who are interested in pursuing more knowledge about Heylal, he appears in the Hebrew Bible. And there are a few mediums who have been successful in channeling him, one such medium is Pamela Aaralyn.

NINE

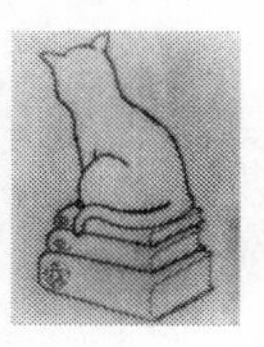

WHO IS YOUR TRIBE?

My partner is Native American and as such, I have gotten a myriad of different reactions to his presence in my life. The most beautiful interactions are from those who listen to his past pain without judgment or defensiveness, and then they ask questions as to how to best approach certain subjects in the future when they should come across other indigenous persons. On one such occasion, when asked "is inquiring which tribe you are from rude?" my partner answered, "No, but, if you want to know how *we* go about asking that question, we say, *Who are your folks*?"

I believe the same respectful manner should be applied when asking yourself the very same question, "Who is your tribe? Who are your folk?"

It doesn't matter if you are new to the Craft or old hat at it. Even if you are a solo practitioner, which most of us are, at least at the beginning, you NEED your community! You also need your soul guides and spirit guides, and you need nature, as much as nature needs you. Witchcraft is about connection; how and why you connect is very much up to you, but making connections is the basis of life, and Witchcraft is life, so, find your peeps. Your heart will be full because of the love your tribe will bring you.

Four basic elements can be found in both the universe itself and humans alike; oxygen, carbon, hydrogen, and nitrogen, meaning we do not merely live in the universe; we are the universe, and the universe is us! It's that simple.

When I was a child I was terrified of open water, which is strange for me as my astrological sun sign and ascendant (rising sign) are in the element of water. One would think I would be completely at home in watery surroundings, but NOPE. When tracing this watery fear, I realized I was afraid of being lost, out to sea, being swept away, even disappearing because of the cruel potential a vast body of water "held" over my tiny four-year-old mind; it had the capability to destroy me!

Sure, nature is beautiful and fierce, and we only need to enter the word tsunami into YouTube to witness the power nature possesses when prompted to act from its untamed origins. However, my fear was enforced by my lack of connection to my surroundings and to my (spiritual) self. A grounded and integrated individual is capable of being respectful of the power of nature and the sea, and still feel no immediate fear from it. But my disconnection from nature never allowed for that respectful connection to take hold; I never felt a part of nature as a child, and I never felt it all around me as others did. I was a willful child, willing myself into and out of every situation I ever encountered. This way of living wasn't very inclusive. I had to learn the difference between my will (the ego), and my soul (the universe).

I remember a spiritual guide once asking me to imagine myself hugging a tree, then melting into it, becoming one with that tree. I tried this exercise, only to be met with panic! Disappearing into a tree trunk sounded like death to me! Of course it did, because the way I was viewing life included the certainty of death. I hadn't begun to see myself as a mystic, or an eternal soul, YET. But, I would.

Now, I know you have been told before that your perspective is everything. How you see the world is creating your reality. Knowing that truism and living it are two very different modes of existence, and how you choose to approach your life is always your business and yours alone. But what if I told you suffering isn't necessary; I mean, NOT AT ALL. You don't need to suffer to be yourself and live the life you want. You don't need to struggle. You don't need to prove yourself. What if I told you what you looked like meant NOTHING! Nothing. No one cares. Looks won't get you what you want; it might get you what you think you need, but that manner of existing will do more to complicate your life and pull you from true and secured happiness. What if I told you your body is a container for light? The light is you. Your soul is eternal, it's energy, it cannot die. It has been through this lifetime and that lifetime, and will probably return again, if you are willing. If you believe any of what is written above, then my question is, what are you waiting for? Life is so short, why wait to love your life and who you already are?

No one should do this work called life alone... No one. That's why finding your folks is imperative. Being around the souls of others who share your frequency is the easiest way to feel as though your life has meaning. How do you meet them? You begin living, truly living, from your heart space, without judgment for yourself or others. I'm not asking you to hug everyone you meet while en-route to the supermarket (although that does sound nice—most people could use a hug). I mean for you to begin seeing yourself as someone outside of yourself, not using your will or your ego to judge and negotiate every scenario in your life.

For example, when attempting to move an object with

your mind, you don't use your will to move it, you manifest this outcome by embracing the process of alchemy, you become the object you wish to move, and then allow it to change you, then a different outcome than the "norm" can take hold. In order to change your life, you can release the necessity to be the change, stop pushing, and just let go. Simple, right? Trust Me, You Got This!

TEN

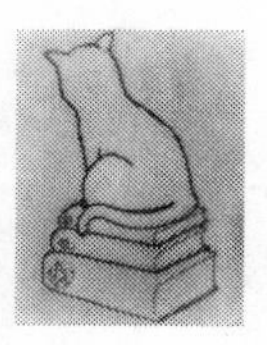

THE INCLUSIVITY OF WITCHCRAFT

The world has set in place many barriers from which we are all judged by.

These methods of categorization are not in keeping with our true natures, which are pure love and elevation. Social constructs aren't profoundly interested in an individuals' need to become the best version of themselves; they exist to keep us in fear and separated, and they have been successful in doing just that for hundreds of years.

One of the many aspects of Witchcraft I adore is the manner in which I can exist without judgment from my immediate and fellow-minded peers. When I am around other Witches, I am in the unique experience of being my true self. I can shed the outer layering of the constructed world that negotiates only within these certain frameworks, sexuality, gender, class, and color.

Each of us, in some capacity or another, have been exposed to the social profiling (for want of a better word) in a very real and painful way, and it is up to us to respect and hold space for each individual's experience of life, and this can be done with no judgment.

Each of us is owed just that, and I have found Witchcraft does honor this basic moral code: WE ARE ALL THE SAME, SO GET OVER YOURSELF IF YOU BELIEVE DIFFERENTLY! Do be respectful about another's experiences and perspectives, and if a specific group of Witches meets your exact (or as close to) experience of life and can offer you a place to be truly seen, and even heal from the crap the outside world hands you, amazing! Go be you!

If anyone, and, I mean anyone, makes you feel incomplete or impresses upon you a shadier version of what Witchcraft stands for, a version that does not uphold the profound oneness of inclusivity, you get the fuck out of where you are and never return to that space. There was never and will never be a doctrine of Witchcraft that pronounces anyone, for whatever reason, better than another. Anyone who does not embrace the basic notion of inclusivity has completely missed the point of Witchcraft, so they should find another way of being that supports their version of a lesser way to be in the world. And honestly, I can only imagine what else they misunderstood about the energy of Witchcraft, so, again, surround yourself with those who have the true knowledge of the beauty and balance of Witchcraft. You owe it to yourself to be treated with kindness, love, respect, and compassion. Why settle for less?

ELEVEN

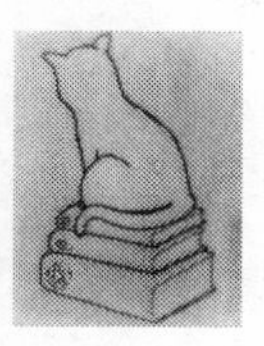

HEALING THE DNA OF WITCHCRAFT

I have been accused of many a thing and way of being in this lifetime of mine; a feminist man-hater or a "man," and everything you can think of that lies in between those two concepts. When people can't define you, or you refuse to define yourself within the very conflicting and narrowing constructs of gender, or any other title, people get very confused, often angry, sometimes even violent.

WELL, FUCK 'EM!!!

What I always loved about Witchcraft is that the knowledge of women is acknowledged, respected, and upheld. I grew up in a Christian faith and was instructed to read the Bible, which always felt male-centered and non-inclusive. It isn't so much to ask that the female form is held and proclaimed as important as their male counterpart; after all, we give life (if we can and/or CHOOSE to), good luck topping that, people!

Generations of women and their kin were murdered by fear parading as colonialism, politics, and intolerant man-made faiths. Witchcraft shares its trauma with many, across nations and other cultures.

Knowledge is in our blood, and so is the pain it caused our ancestors. That pain is still palpable today. We only need to look throughout our immediate environments to see women are still suffering to be heard and seen. Their treatment in society is nowhere near what they deserve, and much of our lineage has been hidden by the wants of men. Well, again, FUCK THE OLD WAY OF BEING! Women all over the planet ARE rising up in solidarity from the #METOO movement, which if nothing else at least provided survivors of sexual abuse, such as myself, the support of others who may have been, until then, victims shrouded in silence. Women's strength and solidarity are being accounted for in all aspects of society, from the entertainment industry to politics. The one understanding I can gather from this new strength of the Goddess Rising is that we are not alone, AND yet, there is still so much we need to do.

We are all made up of feminine and masculine elements. Each of these dimensions of self should to be balanced and healthy if we are to live a glorious life of abundance and beauty. That's where the BOYS come in! Witchcraft has always been about the balance of male and female, and we need you, fellas, and your support to heal. In return, we shall stand in support of your needs as you defend the new version of balance between the sexes, and finally—when we permanently rid ourselves of these restrictions—across genders.

Men have been indoctrinated with (the only word I can think of is…) propaganda regarding the wiles of women and their worth, always in relation to men. This understanding, which no longer serves the collective, should be healed, and the trauma of those before us must be healed. All our ancestors, especially our feminine bloodlines, should be blessed and protected in order for balance to come into being. This can only come to be if the understanding, forgiveness, and respect for knowledge we once held be reinstituted between the male and female legacy.

This act of the divine starts at a basic level; ladies, don't allow men to treat you any less than you deserve—walk away if a lesser situation than you deserve arises. And ladies, we need to support each other, not fall prey to the competitive crap society would have us engage in, so those of us who need support and courage to leave what does not serve them, can pull that energy from the collective and the power of women, and take action to support their highest good in this lifetime. LET'S DO THIS! This beautiful action of healing from past to present is within the lore of Witchcraft, and I trust that every Witch upon this earth is doing their best to serve as a manifestation of profound balance and healing through prayer, Magic, activism, and strength. If you are new to the Craft, welcome; now it's your turn to carry the torch of truth and wisdom.

Blessed Be!

TWELVE

SHOULD WITCHES HAVE CHILDREN?

You fell for that?

Like anyone has the right to answer that question for you.

THIRTEEN

UNLEASHING THE SCREAM

There are many self-help books out there that can instruct you to seek and find your own voice. After all, if you don't speak for yourself, others will.

Those books will give you an overall and much more comprehensive version of healing. This chapter isn't a list of methods to uncover what you stand for and how to project that into the world. I only have one piece of advice. This advice took me all too long to integrate into my own life, but when I did there was a profound shift in my energy and who I began to morph into.

The modern world has only recently started opening up to the necessity of claiming your emotions, but through my travels across lands far and wide I have noticed how many are still extremely uncomfortable when those around us are openly emotional in situations when such openness is not expected. I have even found people are often intimidated by, say, the emotion of anger, seeing it as a personal threat, even when that anger is obviously neither directed at nor has anything to do with the spectator.

However, in direct opposition to what society as a whole may be uncomfortable with, it is my firm belief that gathering your emotions and honoring them is the only way of healing your sorrow and claiming your unique freedom here on earth. There are no escaping emotions; trust me, I was the queen bee when it came to repressing emotions. What I can tell you is the method of repressing becomes very messy when the lid is blown off the emotional hole, and all those years you attempted to run from the emotions you kept so prudently trimmed will cause such a rupture in your psyche you'll be forced to sit, face, and heal, whether you want to or not.

As a consequence of learning to reject my emotions and my voice in social environments, I continued through life never hearing or knowing my pain, never understanding the root of it, and therefore, it was impossible to claim responsibility for it… until one night…

I could tell you that there were a series of intense events that led to the unveiling of my pain, but I would be lying. It was a normal night, it was dark out, and all of a sudden everything rose up inside me, everything I ever wanted to say, express, everything I wanted to hit and hurt because it had hurt me, became clear and I could no longer keep it in. I opened my mouth and I SCREAMED. It was so excruciating to hear my own deep, deep pain. I never knew what it sounded like. It was shocking, violent, even perverse. I was in my backyard within a small compound, which housed my neighbors, who were now front row center to my Hell.

I continued to wail until I reached so far down, any further and I would be screaming for those far beneath the earth. It was more than forty-five minutes before my soul decided I had nothing left to unleash. There were several moments when I was so far within my own hatred of the world that I wasn't sure I would be able to stop screaming, and even if I could, I wasn't sure I would or could return to "normal." What if I couldn't put myself back together after this event? I wasn't even sure the screams were my own. What if it wasn't my own voice? What if I was possessed? I could feel the pain, and I knew the pain was mine, but this voice, where did it come from? I'd never heard it before, so, perhaps this wasn't actually happening. If it weren't for my partner silently watching (for the cops) as I pushed up too many years of being silent for too long, I wouldn't have believed I was capable of such an action, but I had a witness...

The next day I had bloody and swollen knuckles—apparently, I needed to punch something too; unfortunately, it was a brick wall that held together my back yard (note to self, buy professional punching bag!) I was also left with a sore throat and the fact that I couldn't close my hands without searing pain. Both these inflictions proved to me I had taken it upon myself to finally let go on my own terms.

And it felt FUCKING AMAZING! Yes, I was embarrassed; I had been conditioned to have that response to owning my forceful and aggressive method of unleashing, but I didn't care. I wore my embarrassment like a champion fighter. In one night I had connected to a voice of certainty, of strength. Yes, it held pain at its core, but it held wisdom and life, and no one would ever be able to silence me again; I wouldn't let them, even if it cost me my life. So my advice to you is know your pain, and, especially, for all you ladies out there, you need to hear your pain. SCREAM it out. You need to hear it. You deserve to. Scream until you have nothing left, then if you need to, gather your strength and scream again. As long as you hear your own voice, your own pain, you will connect with it, you will feel your soul sitting quietly at the end of your release, ready to be reclaimed. Scream together, or go it alone. If you have a car, drive out where you are alone except for the non-judgmental support of nature, then unleash your beautiful pain, until you feel yourself come back to you.

I promise you will never be the same!

FOURTEEN

HOW DEMONS CAN HELP YOU RECLAIM YOUR SANITY

Oh yes, you just read the chapter heading correctly. Demons can help you reclaim your sanity and your soul. There's a profound and direct correlation between freedom from fear and demons, and here it is...

The modern world has succumbed to the notion of absolutes, one of them being good and evil. We are witness to these opposing concepts every day. We are also judged and reduced to living within their parameters. It is my belief that if we choose one of these "sides" of consciousness, we are reducing ourselves to nothing more than a fraction of what we actually are and can achieve in this lifetime. Fear is a great organizer, and choosing between the polarizing concepts of good and evil keeps you fearful. When a person is fearful they are less lightly to question, deliver, overcome and recreate. Well, you were born to do the opposite of living a life where you add to the outmoded duality of thinking that at its best produces more fear and sets the foundation for miscommunication.

In truth, there is so much relevant knowledge that can be

gained from the study of demons and demonology. After all, knowledge is power. Once you have procured some knowledge of demons you may not hold as much fear in your heart when being faced with a situation where you may come across one or two.

I'm not suggesting you grab a Ouija board and seek out every demon who will interact with you. I'm suggesting the opposite—I am suggesting you are conscious enough to understand that demons are an extension of yourself, a facet of reality that can and should be respected and integrated, not feared.

I'll give you an example of how an incomplete knowledge of demonology keeps us ignorant of the facts. Let's talk about poor Pazuzu. This demon is, in actuality, the king of demons. Pazuzu has been demonized (yes, I went there!) and inaccurately represented in *The Exorcist,* first a book then a film directed by William Friedkin. The truth of Pazuzu's presence is that he protects children and women against lower entities and other demonic presences. His (now infamous) part dog, part human (on occasion pictured with a face of part lion part human) was, and still is, worn around the necks of pregnant women to protect their unborn child. Would this king of demons have possessed a twelve-year-old girl, with or without her proclivity towards using the Ouija board? FUCK NO! There have been *Exorcist* film fan theorists who have suggested that Pazuzu only possessed the child protagonist in an to attempt to protect her from the actual demons that were responsible for her possession, and the Catholic church's intervention, which resulted in Pazuzu's expulsion, only served to exacerbate the situation, resulting in deaths, including the death of Father Karras. This theory is much closer in accuracy than the intrusive version of events rendered in the aforementioned film.

I believe if more watchers were exposed to the above fan theory regarding Pazuzu they would be less affected by the underlying message *The Exorcist* carries; all demons should be feared, and humans (especially young females) can be readily violated by the power that demons possess. This fearful approach toward "understanding" demons does more to sell movie tickets and keep society small and silent than it does to recreate the actuality of demonic presence in the modern world.

Compassion is at the heart of discovery, and we can move into the state of compassion only when we move past the limitations of fear. Ironically, *The Exorcist* redeems itself and offers an example of demonic compassion within its newly developed television script, which first graced our screens in 2016. The first season of the television adaptation of *The Exorcist* saw Father Marcus visit a nunnery where Mother Bernadette's version of exorcism involved silent expressions of acknowledgment and compassion, which countered the benign and common vision of a male priest wildly screaming verses of the Bible in a forced approach to driving out what isn't wanted and is, therefore, misunderstood. For Mother Bernadette, silence and beauty free from the confines of fear allowed for acceptance; within that acceptance, whatever is misunderstood is no longer denied, and there is no longer a quest for power, one over another. There is no need to denounce one to gain victory, a useless, and outmoded approach to the exorcism process. Mother Bernadette's power was pure beauty at its best and demonstrated that, yet again, the vision and wisdom of women when adhered to pushes new versions of how to approach the understanding of evil without exploiting it as a method to heighten our relationship to fear.

If you want to live outside of fear's reign over society, I

suggest you learn about what lives in the darkness. If you do, they will stay in the dark no longer, and your fear of demons and yourself will morph into understanding and wisdom. New beginnings originate from new understandings of the ancient.

FIFTEEN

THE FEMININE REINVENTION OF POWER

The quote by Eleanor Roosevelt, *"well-behaved women seldom make history"* holds true, even today. Women live in an earthly environment where their mind, rights, even their bodies are spoken for by those who have been given no reason to approve of her power and presence. Witchcraft holds the opposite format in its approach to females and their inner-strength, which is why it is a light-filled and beautiful path to take in this lifetime. So, how does a Witch of any age or race reclaim her power from a world that has yet to seek mercy for killing her great (x 10) grandmother?

Well, you begin the life of non-apology. That's the way forward. Now to be clear, if you fuck up and it causes pain to another, do the right thing, but, I know you will, so, back to my point…

The essence of the non-apology concept comes from taking NO, and I mean NO responsibility for anyone else's actions. It means living as you want without explaining yourself. It means your version of responsibility is just that; yours! It means you push to the front of the line if that is what you desire, and never hold yourself back from what needs to be said. It means not explaining your behavior, even if others believe it is off or even "immoral." Words have power. Use the word "sorry" with intention; keep it for special occasions, only for when it is truly necessary to utter.

As an example of how we are conditioned, I urge you to watch how many times you apologize in a day. Record the findings; you might be surprised. No more apologizing for daring to exist! How many times did someone bump into you and *you* apologized? How many times do you say sorry for taking too long, or taking up too much time? Again, your results could reveal some very interesting ways you communicate your power, or compromise it, without realizing. We all engage in this behavior. How many times do you witness other women saying sorry to you when you bump into *them* with your cart at the supermarket?

Simple observations and shifts in perceptions can change your inner power; sometimes less is more.

How many times have you been projected upon by someone else's pain, and still you've apologized, because that someone was angry at you? THAT'S NOT OK! You're much more than another's projection, so much more...

It is up to us to support and provide freedom for ourselves, each other and the next generation; it will not be freely given. Our freedom is wild, and the feminine spirit is glorious, largely undocumented, and free. Being your wild self shouldn't be seen as bold, but it often is. Bold behavior is often reserved for those who are considered either deserving of its delights because of the courage they hold within, or those who are considered too aberrant to naturally fit within a prescribed version of femininity.

To each and every beautiful Witch, YOU take that space and power you deserve and don't apologize for your truthful and profound strength in finding and unleashing your own true voice. Remember you are not alone.

That's one of the pleasures of being one of us.

We are everywhere.

So grateful for you all.

SIXTEEN

THE VOID

I know the title of this chapter is somewhat ominous, but, in truth, the process of the *void* is Magical in its own right. It is said you only completely die once—you keep dying until you are free to allow something new to grow.

I never really grasped the understanding of living in the moment, free from the whims of my ego. It seemed an unfocused way to live, and, dare I say it, almost uneventful, a boring existence. I believed yogis could and should achieve this thoughtful method of approaching life because they lived on mountain tops. Outside of the modern world, they could afford for this higher vibration to take hold. I, however, did not live outside of the modern world. I had rent and bills to pay, so, this method of integration should stay beyond me.

I already understood that healing was a profoundly messy occurrence, a method of trying to grab at the ebb and flow of life; a process that may never be over for me in this lifetime. I was someone who loved new beginnings but hated transitions and avoided them at all costs, so it took me many years to be open enough to fall into my *void*, a place where I initially believed I was dead with no guarantee of resurrection.

I never envisioned that there was a place beyond time and space where life as I knew it came to a complete standstill, so slow in its relation to me that I could see, hear, and feel every personal decision I had ever made. I could feel these tenuous connections to who I believed I was. Every thought and judgment I had was just a reflection of how I saw myself. I could feel that small box I had put myself into, and yet I expected others to see beyond my own self-imposed limitations. I had been lazy, untrue and too frightened to rise up from my circumstances.

The universe had given me this gift, which I refer to as the *void*, but, in truth, it cannot be named. There were pronounced signs of this process entering into my life. Everything that was familiar and everyone I believed was kin fell away from my life, sometimes through ridiculous means that made no logical sense at the time, but it was the universe clearing away what and who was connected to my past, not my future.

Because of my belief in other realms, when faced with the *void* I did not run; I breathed and allowed myself to stay and watch as an observer. The fear of creating a new beginning, leaving behind that which I believed I had spent many years achieving, transformed into a new opportunity to begin again. I had entered into other realms many times—practicing Magic afforded me this opportunity, but I had never experienced these other realms from the inside out; I had only ever been a visitor.

I could actually hear the seeds I had planted, now growing, and yet I was in no hurry to see them bloom; nature has its own flourishing process. This new understanding had previously been completely beyond me as I had always been in a hurry, always busy, making plans, making lists, even the (hopefully) ever-present needing to become spirituality awakened was on a list of things to do.

The Craft arose and thrives within its own nature, and it works beyond what we perceive as "real life." The path of healing works in the same way.

If you allow yourself to walk into that place of supposed darkness, at first the intrusion of loneliness might affect you. But I believe if you move beyond who you believe you are and drop all pretenses, you have the chance to touch the essence of what Witchcraft truly is. Try approaching the process of the *void* with no judgment for yourself; just allow the emotions to show themselves in this sacred space.

My processing within the essence of the *void* included no longer wanting to be an "upstanding" citizen of the world. Instead, I now lived to tell and record the relevancy of limitlessness. I always knew there was more to life than achieving, but I never felt the momentum of true progress before my relationship to nothingness. Having your truth be a palpable presence breaks you from the circle of conformity.

Your belief in yourself and the all that the Craft can be, if used wisely and without fear, will no doubt bring you to your own version of the *void*, or whatever you choose to call it, and that's an amazing feat. That's where you'll find your lifeline, soul mates, true desires, and the blessed guides who will aid your soul's development far quicker and with far more lucid results than the human world will ever be able to offer you.

SEVENTEEN

SHAME, FEAR'S INSIDIOUS SIBLING. IT WILL RULE YOU NO MORE

When I was a child I would hear my mother say, "that-so-and-so (she could not for the life of her remember anyone's name, including mine!) has no shame, none at all." I can honestly say I never fully felt the profoundness of that sentence, not until my own shame, which was so deeply rooted it felt as though it belonged to everyone else, came crashing into my fortress of feelings with no forewarning. Moving through the *void* can be a beautiful experience of hope, the promise of the brand new, but, what if we only experience moments of the promises the *void* can provide? How, on this green earth, do we fully integrate into our future free selves without the influence of the past? How do we not slip back into the crevices of our own darkness again?

Owning then releasing our shame.

No one is born with shame; it's a learned response that is pushed through every aspect of society, from our upbringing to our social systems, school, work, and our sense of play. Most of us have touched elements of our shame, but very few know how deep-rooted it is and to what degree it influences our decisions, our lives, and our ability to love ourselves and others fully.

For me, moving into the *void* was a necessary part of my healing process, simply because it allowed for the abstract parts I had no interest in being faced with to show me why I wasn't the person I wanted to be yet. Once within the *void*, my shame presented itself as an old weakness. That's all I was told it was; "everyone has weaknesses; it's normal; it's the human experience... you are, after all, human, aren't you?"

"Weakness" or *shame*, as I now know it to be, had me believe that my natural and constant state was to be small, to renounce my own true desires in situations. My entire life was filtered through shame's dislike of my own yet-to-be-claimed strength. As a consequence of living this way, I constantly mistook other's manipulative practices for an authoritative presence I should adhere to. I surrounded myself with those who believed they were superior to most around them, yet they were often the souls who needed the most healing. Those persons were often quick to judge behavior that when turned toward me, triggered my shame so profoundly I fell into the trap of disappearing from my own body and unable to take any accountability for what would transpire; I gave other's judgments power over my own circumstances. I approached my life without the realization that the very people who I believed "had my back" were the people inciting the noxious situations in my life. Shame controlled everything and everyone I allowed into my life, and set up a wall of constant drama of which served to highlight the energy of dysfunction that was desperately calling to be healed.

It was only when I asked the question, "Where the Hell did *I* go?" that I was given the answer, "you gave yourself up to shame." I had given myself up so many times without knowing the process of what I had entered into that I couldn't feel myself fully in my body anymore. It was as if a part of me had left and did not know how to return, and without my missing pieces I would remain somewhat at the mercy of those who carried the burden of shame also; I would never be free from it or the judgments of others.

Tracing how shame had paved the way for the slow yet steady decline of my inner strength was painful, but in doing so, I began to hold the belief that what awaited me was true freedom from my life's captors.

My first approach to integrating my shame was to claim my "weaknesses," which equated to embracing my naivety and vulnerability; two modes of being that are NOTHING to be ashamed of! I was, and had never been, "weak." When claiming control over my own vulnerability, which was invigorating, I discovered another aspect of my soul that had been so neglected they had gone into hiding—my pure, sweet, inner child.

I was too busy trying to survive that I didn't give my inner-child the appropriate recollection. As such, they pushed and pulled, displaying their wants and needs, perhaps causing the very situations that would in time force me to reclaim my soul.

There were times when I needed to hear my own voice and pain to be able to heal, but for diluting my shame I took a different route. In honor of my broken, yet soon to be discovered inner child, I gathered what strength I had and took that strength, and presented it into another space and time for the process of healing. Those of you who do Magic know that there are other realms and other realities, elementals, guides, beauty and divinity that are only a moment's call away. If being human caused this much pain, trying to heal from the limitations of the human realm made no sense to me or to my inner child. I choose the quietness of the wild or animals, both of this earth, and beyond. I offered my pain—

my shame—up to deities, to guides, to the loving energy of Source, and they gladly took it from me and transformed it back into the light and fire it began as. If the concept of other realms began to strike me as too fanciful, I imagined myself as an owl, night-bound, shameless, and powerful. The owl has no use for shame, so why should I?

I needed my inner-child to direct this version of my healing experience, and they did not disappoint. Not only could I grasp the ineffectuality of shame, but I also began to witness what beauty existed when incorporating a child-like existence into the matter of becoming ME. Living without the consequences of shame means to live a life free from the fear that your human self will never be enough, a silly little lie shame desperately needs you to believe. You tell shame you have a new path now; the path of unparalleled freedom!

EIGHTEEN

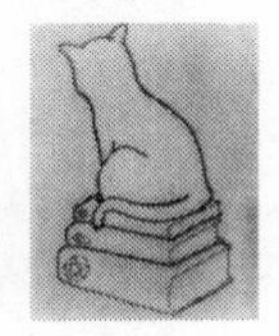

THE MUNDANE WORLD VERSUS THE BEAUTY OF WHAT LIES AHEAD

As humans, we are born into a world with a beginning, a middle, and an end. What I originally loved about this world was that rules and regulations existed. I know it's ridiculous that I am saying this, as I have spent most of my life breaking rules. However, rules gave me a sense of comfort at first. I believed there were parameters from which I could never fall away from or out of.

As I matured, the concept of rules became cumbersome and heavy. I began to feel the pressure of them. I, like many, became a witness to the select few violating the protection that rules should have offered. My soul started to suffer as my pain body took on the suffering of others; I had tapped into the collective pain here on earth. When I was twenty-four my body could take on no more darkness and I broke. I broke wide open. I felt as though there was nowhere to hide, and I couldn't run, as I was acutely aware I would be taking myself everywhere I went.

I wouldn't love any aspect of my "brokenness" for many years, but the one understanding the experience left me with was the clear knowledge that my pain body, which was full and now lethal to the touch, could be traced back to specific timelines where I had created different versions of myself.

As a consequence of this way of being, I lived a fractured life for many years. One aspect of me adhered to the concept of time, and the other disbelieved in the process of time, as it is non-linear and only integrated into the human world. A part of myself judged my life by the passing of time, and I set up personal conquests around the concept that time offered, and if I didn't "achieve" them I berated myself, moving me further and further away from loving my life and living a full and meaningful existence.

This time-based existence also showed me how much disdain I had for corrupt political alliances. I could feel the collective energy of the self-imposed ruling class no longer served us all; they represented and served the individual. And when seeking freedom and healing from this version of living I found normal modes of healing set up within the boundaries of the human world; therapy and suchlike useless to me. They were a reflection of the outer problem; they also represented the individualistic mindset, not the collective.

To heal, I began to seek out the many other versions of existence. There were many very painful understandings about myself I had to shed before I could do this; it was imperative I release the labels I had taken on: victim, woman, lesser than, not enough, non-intellectual, emotional, crazy, fucked up, recluse, incomplete, and wrong. I needed to embrace the fact that if I worked within the framework of these labels, they just might kill my human body.

Then there were other cuts needing to be made. The concepts of right and wrong, the dualistic thinking that no longer served, as everyone has their own version of the truth. I had set limitations on my soul. I needed to reintroduce the fact that anything was possible—I mean anything; beyond my social conditioning, anything could be achieved if I believed. These understandings brought me to a huge life-returning realization. My inner compass could no longer rely on the opinions of others, neither good nor bad, as they meant nothing.

All the suffering I had put myself through was mine. I had created the pain, and sometimes it had arisen from the need to incorporate the opinions of others, those I had trusted to tell me the truth. But their truth was constructed from their own relationship to their pain, and so the endless circle of humanness moved me sideways, never forward. If I was to cut through my circle of pain I had created and stop reliving my same agony, I would need to break up with the limited mindset I had inherited, not chosen. To be human did not mean I should have to compromise my beauty, my expansiveness, my freedom. Healing is a process with no limitations if you are open to the concept that the human world is merely one illusion of thought that is not the only container for your (hopefully unbridled) life.

NINETEEN

THE LIMITLESSNESS OF ABUNDANCE

Each of us is taught, to some degree, to believe that we are merely human; earthlings, one-dimensional thinkers, we're here one minute, then moving out of this existence quicker than a flash of light. What if we were taught from birth that our soul is completely autonomous, infinite, free, and permeates every level of existence from trees, park benches, fellow humans, and everyone and everything in between? If you had parents who taught you this freedom-based truth, rock on! Go call them and let them know they are indeed rock stars of the spiritual realm! However, for most of us being reared in an environment that taught limitlessness isn't an everyday occurrence, and, even if it was, unfortunately our society, and many of the single digit god believing religions, don't support this sense of self-worth. But no matter, you know the truth limitlessness has to offer. I know you've always felt it. But now comes the important question. How do we live out our limitless thought process every day and reclaim our life, light and, find our soul's purpose—which is to be free and happy, living in unison with our highest sense of self?

Well, the first thing I'm going to tell you is that what others have advised in the past may not work for you, so feel free to ignore that advice. If the mainstream advice does hit home for you, WHOOPEE! It just didn't for me. I don't know how many times I have been told to visualize what I wanted and it will come to me—"fake it till I made it." But what if all you are doing is just faking it, and all you are visualizing is what you believe you want or should have?

There are many times where I can recall visualizing something and the outcome did occur, and then I was forced to live through the existence of it, and I was miserable! And I did spend much of my life faking it, not knowing who or what I supposed to be making it for.

Living a limitless existence is just that; there's no real need to visualize, as your whole life is a series of visualizations, ideas, and formulations all designed to support your highest ideals. There's no need to fake your life when you deem to live outside of that box you have been assigned from childhood.

Abundance WILL be attracted to you and will come into your life in profound and lasting ways if you do one thing—believe you deserve everything you ask for. It seems simple, but many don't believe they deserve love, to be happy, or to have money.

Money isn't a reality. It's a piece of paper. Why is it you do not believe you deserve paper coming in and supporting your highest visions for this lifetime of yours? Money is not something to be gained, something always outside of yourself, external to your experience of it. If you have this relationship to money you may always struggle to attract it. Money has a clear and beautiful energy. It can be both repelled or attracted to your relationship to the concept of it. If you are trying to make money while hosting a fearful life, or if you remain uncertain whether you can even attract (as you never have been able to before), then why would it come to you? It's like inviting someone over for dinner with shit stains all over the invitations, and asking them to bring their own food! Would you show up to the address on the invitation for "dinner"? Nope. And neither will money.

For all you wonderful altruistic folks out there doing amazing work, *there is nothing wrong with wanting money or to be successful doing what you do.* If your core belief does not support you being successful, release that belief and reprogram your energy with a limitless thinking process. I love money; it represents freedom. It gives you the freedom and the means to help and support others in ways you wouldn't be able to without the presence of that beautiful green paper. However, many (including my past myself) hold the unconscious belief that money is dirty, or that they should work very hard to gain favor with it. Perhaps being impoverished will keep you safe from the responsibility of being out in the world. There are many different reasons why you might not believe you deserve abundance, or once it starts to arrive, push it away. Clear, clear, clear, so you will be able to clearly attract it.

Money isn't complicated. It's made up of elemental energy. That's a fun frequency to work with; it's the frequency shared by fairies. This frequency is attracted to laughter, to play, and belief. If you hold the same frequency as money you will no longer need to attract it because it will seek *you* out.

All you Witches, solo practitioners or beautiful coven members (or both); you have an understanding of energy, its ebb, and flow. You have the subtlety of mind needed to conjure and create your belief in love and the limitless mindset. Anoint yourself with the knowledge of unconditional love. Spellwork, truth, and community will bring you closer and support you in this journey of shedding and coming back to the infinite and remaining there.

Remember, sometimes the only road forward means to do nothing but rise from the old. The universe will deliver all the abundance you deserve, more even… as always, never settle for less.

TWENTY

THERE ARE NO HEALERS, ONLY WITNESSES

The world is filled with energy healers. It is my belief the world requires these energies, and that they exist in this time and space because there is much healing to be administered to each individual, their bloodlines, and Mother Earth, the beautiful place that holds our pain; she perhaps requires the most healing. It is my belief every free-thinking individual has the capacity for healing themselves and others on a profound level. I believe that statement to be a fact. Sometimes healing can occur in a simple day-to-day manner; promoting compassion through a heartfelt smile. For someone who has not been exposed to the purity that compassion has to offer, this seemingly simple gesture can become a catalyst for freedom. Or, perhaps, your abilities will take shape in a container that has a more defined purpose, spellwork, herbalism, mediumship, business icon (go you!) or channeling; these being just a few examples.

Regardless of how you choose to manifest your abilities to induce change and healing in this lifetime—being a good friend, or opening a business to promote healing—do remember the one golden rule. You are not the *Healer,* you are merely the *Witness*. The beautiful soul who came to you in need is the only healer in the room. Energy healers are here on earth to ground into their own power and to help others to do the same, utilizing every system of support possible. Supporting and witnessing another's healing is a simple yet Magical process that loses its Magic if we claim healing as something "we did."

There can be no ego in energy healing. The point of the healing process is that we are working outside of the ego and directing another beyond the limitations the fragile ego relies upon to exist. The need for recognition is fleeting and will only serve to keep you small. Ego-based mystical work will never serve you, and your ego-based thoughts will be sensed by others. So leave your ego at home; or, better still, work with your beautiful ego's protective energy and reassign them to another, less presumptuous level of your consciousness. The ego isn't evil, but they aren't a necessary confidant once you begin to live a truthful, in-line-with-your-soul-life.

As most of us have never been privy to true acceptance, just bringing in this energy for another can shift a soul's recognition back to who they really are: a being of light, capable of limitless thinking! So remember your quest for beauty; be there as a catalyst for change. The sky is the limit for all who transcend their pasts. Being a witness for this vision of perfection in another is what keeps my soul from slipping back into the small box the world once had me believe I needed to live and die in.

I love my life, and if you don't love yours yet, you will.

Always seek out your intuition's verdict on which energy alchemist you should work with. Trust me, your intuition really does know what's best for you, so trust yourself!

TWENTY-ONE

A CHANNELED MESSAGE FROM HECATE

I first came across Hecate while mediating. I was enlisted in an energy alchemist course at the time which encouraged seeking out your spiritual guides, and I certainly did I find them.

At first, her appearance was alarming. She commanded my attention, a fierce entity, clouded in smoke, and surrounded by allies; spiders. I'm a fan of arachnids, but, even so, this vision was unnerving. Her energy was palpable, as were her messages. It was only after some research I discovered that this iconic version of her was not uncommon. Hecate's presence has been a consistent force in my life. These are her words… from her to you:

Even in the most difficult times, the darkness around you contains light. Neither can exist without each other, so there is no need for fear. What the soul wants most is to be free, but the human mind needs to play a part in this process, control this process. The way to true freedom is to live beyond the mind's need to be involved in who you believe yourself to be. Staying true to the gift of life will bring your soul much further than the need to accomplish. The world has seen too many conquerors, the universe needs you to exist everywhere without claiming territories and building boundaries, that only works to secure and impoverish the soul's development. Do you see that true freedom and your mind's need to be sensible do not match your heart's desire which is simply to be allowed to love, love in its highest capacity?

Unconditional love exists only when the mind has surrendered its power over to the highest source there is, YOU. Human life is not for the timid. I have always known this to be true. Minds are corrupted and false truths work hand in hand with fear to bring you further from your own power. Constructed truths in the form of religion cannot replace the fundamentals of unconditional love. Peace, truth, and light come to you only when you are open to receiving it. It is your choice to live in fear and stay afraid of the darkness. But parts of your soul reside in the darkness; will you not care enough for your soul to retrieve them and bring them to the light? We cannot teach you your divinity and give you the strength you need to be your true self; you must request this need throughout your own soul, throughout existence, and throughout the kingdom of darkness, then we can aid your brokenness, the beauty of it will shine, so you can have a record of the experience of being human before you resume your purpose, which is to exist in accord with everything and everyone. There is much to do and there is little action needed to pull your soul into its true existence. Why do you wait?

TWENTY-TWO

REDEFINING THE FEMININE FROM THE WORDS OF A GODDESS

HECATE II

After channeling the previous chapter, Hecate unleashed these words upon me. I was also informed that the word channeling isn't in line with her thoughts on communication. Merely dropping into the frequency of the entity who wishes to communicate is enough to bring energy and words forth…

Human fields of existence have separated the masculine and the feminine, taking one for pleasure and seeking authority through the voice of the other. Neither exists in unity without the other, and yet a full existence is expected to be lived without healing what has been done to separate. Nothing thrives in the effects of separation, nothing can grow and sustain good health without the understanding that completeness exists only when two parts are free to express themselves, and free to exist in harmony with their underlying nature. Pleasure has been disbanded to make room for severity, and for what? What did you gain by shutting down your soul's need to feel ecstasy? You were born to experience pleasure. You are here to understand the fundamentals of unity, of trust and to feel the experience of this through your physical body, your mind, and your soul. We did not want or require you to live without. That is not the way.

There has been much talk about reclaiming what has been lost, but you cannot claim the loss of self; you participated in allowing to be pulled from your true self, a part of you continues in this sickness.

No reclaiming is necessary, it is for you to breathe back into you the life and power that was separated in the quest for authority, a quest that left everyone who participated weak and fragile, male and female. Forgiveness exists for all those brave enough to seek out a new way of standing in their own light. Being united, both systems of thought, masculine and feminine are possible now. The integrity of wholeness could not have sustained itself before now; you were not able to hold the brightness of all that you can be when both aspects of self are unified.

Pure and unconditional love that paves the way for forgiveness, the need to forgive the human plight for power, can hold the space for true unity, and those who do not wish to be a part of this true identity, this progress, will stay within the confines of fear within their own darkness falling away from the new way of being.

To seek the frequency of the new, vibrant and restated love for the feminine; beauty that transcends the human mind is to bathe in its light and to be at one with the power of femininity. Nothing fair or reasonable exists without the feminine, and nothing lasts or conquerors without the protection of the masculine. True unity is found in each soul who seek it, and they will spark a new light in those who carry the codes for unification. All pain is lost when unity is felt and known in each soul. This is our gift to you, a precious gift of balance, no transcendence can be found without the reinstating of balance.

TWENTY-THREE

THE ILLUSION OF STORYTELLING

I was no stranger to make-believe worlds and trying on new and improved identities growing up. I can recall with acute clarity the time I brought friends home from school to meet E.T., who was, according to my make-shift but already well-defined world, living in my house. Behind my bunk bed, to be specific. I also hold a very real memory of meeting Santa Claus after he shimmied down our chimney on a cold and dark night in the fourth year of my existence. Those memories and the experience of them are so real that they are more vivid and alive to me then my day-to-day life. It took me several years to piece together that I couldn't have actually met Santa Claus as my childhood home did not have a chimney; I had made over my house to fit my childhood delusions!

When I was older I experimented with the need for different realities and different versions of my story thus far. I constantly shifted my identity, my name, and homeland, trying new versions of me on, shedding the old ones like snake skins. It was around this time I began to notice those around me often had explosive reactions to my shifting and changing my supposed identity. On such occasions I would be called a fake, or a spray on, unreal. These manufactured responses often insinuated I was a liar, that I shouldn't be trusted. I was constantly confused by these reactions. Trying on new identities seemed harmless, but there were many who truly believed in the need for the story behind our identity and my seemingly frivolous attempt to leave mine behind posed a threat to their understanding of the human existence.

Shifting and changing realities, version of events, and life-changing memories didn't bring me any closer to the freedom I so desperately wanted. I could become a different incarnation of self, but this process never accurately allowed for the space to become limitless or touch the limitlessness that promised true freedom.

The self-constructed entity that is you has a name, a personal history, a journey of your soul bound by memories, heartaches, and victories. If one releases all of what they believe they are, do they truly exist? Can we exist beyond our need for human individuality?

I would not have had the courage to even attempt to answer these questions if Witchcraft had not been a part of my soul's makeup. Witchcraft as an identity exists outside of what is considered by the masses as "normal." The need or the desire to remake yourself outside of a system of belief that may consider you already somewhat aberrant is the Witch's gift to the art of healing, and it is this truism that allowed me the courage to move beyond the notion of self to a place where there was nothing, only simple, quiet manifestations. I relinquished my attachment to my own drama, my need to be right.

I never understood that true freedom came from leaving behind ALL the versions of self to form a new reality, one that didn't include anything familiar or personal to my actual life, as these were clouded versions of what I could expect to become.

There are many illusions we as human have adopted as truth. And there is perhaps no greater illusion than who we are as a living entity from the moment we exist on this earth. Each of us decodes our worth and dictates who and why we love based on the illusion of being "ourselves." Our very sense of self is often constructed from perceived slights or wrongdoings that have occurred against us, when in truth events that take place in our energy field are a reflection of the darkness that exists everywhere, and, therefore, may not have originated from our own source of pain. Living free means just that. It's a non-constructed, fluid existence that has no story and does not seek to find it through the need for a human identity, so maybe it is time to lose it.

TWENTY-FOUR

TRANSPOSING THE NEED FOR WARRIORSHIP

I grew up falling in love with the idea of the female warrior —the legend that illuminated her, the energy and the wisdom she possessed. From a small age I believed I would grow into my own version of the beloved female warrior archetype, full of the wisdom that had graced my screen for over twenty years in various forms. OK, mainly Wonder Woman. It never occurred to me I could become all that I wanted and desired without the need for warriorship. There was another way. I did not need to fight to be seen, and I definitely did not need to guard and protect the beauty of what I could and would become.

I spent so much of my life pushing to get ahead, doing what I believed I must to get me there. But it would take me such a long time to ask myself what it was I truly wanted; *to slow down, to just be able to feel and love everything without the need for judgment.*

I took my own sweet time to be able to confidently state, I NO LONGER GIVE A SHIT, and to mean it; a process of spiritual development that I feel is as vibrant and as necessary as breathing. It took me even longer to walk away from each circumstance without needing approval outside of myself, knowing any path I chose was brand new and I possessed no vision of how it would end.

The final barrier, and perhaps the most important to comprehend, was to completely embrace vulnerability and to make a home for faith. So I no longer needed to plan for the worst just in case of failure. I could now be sure that if I embraced who I was, free from everything I once allowed to define me, movement existed and its direction, although undefined, was always forward. Failure as a concept was no longer any use to me. There were only experiences to be had, and these experiences did not need to be arranged by the polarizing right or wrong, success or failure module that once plagued my life.

A limitless existence is a life full of infinite possibilities beyond what you even conceived for yourself; you are a gift to yourself and the world. So, as the title suggests, I transposed the need to be a warrior and instead, I embraced the realization that instead of fighting to the top of my life, I could give myself the love and peacefulness needed to safely merge into MY version of the sacred Goddess…

"A goddess is a woman who emerges from deep within herself. She is a woman who has honestly explored her darkness and learned to celebrate her light. She is a woman who is able to fall in love with the magnificent possibilities within her. She is a woman who knows of the Magic and mysterious places inside her, the sacred places that can nurture her soul and make her whole. She is a woman who radiates light. She is magnetic." ~ Author Unknown

TWENTY-FIVE

AND THEN IT WAS OVER...

Moving graciously and beautifully into your limitless self is the most significant gift you can give the world. The universe will support you in every aspect of this journey; you are never alone. True healing will occur from understanding and believing in this simple, and (let's face it) obvious truth.

Nature-based paths and ways of being—like those adopted within the Witchcraft community, to name but a few—are in natural alignment with the ebb and flow of nature, her cycles of life, and her gentle wisdom.

This book wasn't written exclusively for Witches, although you all have a special place in my heart. Besides, most of us are Witches—born free, strong, with a profound respect for Mother Earth and her wisdom.

It is my hope that my story proved to you that you are not alone and that we are all here to assist each other in breaking out of the pain loop, a process of the ego which can no longer support our soul's spiritual development.

Brand new beginnings are upon us if we Rise Together and never forget, we are ALL made from STARDUST, not coal, so now is the time to live as such.

Blessed be, my sweets! Blessed be,
The Merry Way Witch.

HEALING AND WITHCRAFT

"It is up to us to support and provide freedom for ourselves, each other and the next generation; it will not be freely given. Our freedom is wild, and the feminine spirit is glorious, largely undocumented, and free."

Healing and Witchcraft in a Conformist World is a personal account of healing through the essence of Witchcraft in a world that has yet to embrace the bold power of the feminine.

The Merry Way Witch delivers a powerful journey of freedom and inclusiveness asserting herself beyond the subjectivity of the patriarchy.

ABOUT THE AUTHOR

The Merry Way Witch is a fiction writer, freelance metaphysical writer, and creator of her own destiny. She resides in New Mexico, where she is currently working on several creative projects that she hopes will change the world, in small yet profound ways.

Keith Rock is a Native American contemporary artist originally from the vastness of Montana. He currently resides in Santa Fe, New Mexico, where he works in his studio by day and howls at the moon by night.

You can find The Merry Way Witch at www.rebeccatroyearthangelalchemist.com or on Instagram @rebecca_alchemywitch.

And reach Keith Rock at www.keithrock.com or on Instagram @mr.keithrock.

Made in the USA
San Bernardino, CA
02 August 2020

76357194R00051